HEALTHY GLUTEN FREE RECIPES

For Electric Pressure Cookers

Table of Contents

Introduction

Modern day pressure cookers are a great way to prepare meals. It's fast, easy and clean. You can cook just about anything in them and save lots of time over conventional cooking. The recipes in this book are healthy and gluten free. They contain no wheat, sugar or any "processed foods" and they are paleo compliant.

I have been experimenting with different recipes and ways to use my pressure cooker and I have found one method that is quick, easy, and fun and the results are delicious. Its PRESSURE COOKING WRAPPED IN FOIL. You can prepare packets of all in one meals very fast and easy. The best results are with chicken breasts preferably boneless, skinless and split. I use organic chicken from Whole Foods or individually wrapped, all natural chicken breast made by Natures Promise (Purdue has a similar product) that are about 6 oz. each. You can use any  brand that you like (if you are going Paleo then pasteurized chicken, grass feed beef and naturally caught fish are the way to go. I have included several of these types of recipes and instructions in this cookbook.

Another pressure cooking process is fusion cooking. Place the meat or poultry directly into liquid, water with spices added, beer, wine, or any other flavored liquid. The flavor of the liquid will be infused into whatever is cooking under the pressure.

Then there is the steaming method. Place the food to be cooked in a steamer basket or rack or trivet so that the food does not touch the liquid but gets steam cooked from the pressurized liquid.

As you use your pressure cooker you will realize its diverse uses and have fun experimenting!

The recipes in this book were developed and cooked with a Wolfgang Puck Bistro Elite Pressure Cooker. It is a simple cooker with a timer and three settings, heat, cook and warm. If you are familiar with the cooking times of your pressure cooker, compare with the timing and settings of the recipes and adjust if necessary. If you are new to cooking with an electric pressure cooker, you can check the manufacturer's manual and compare cooking times and settings. You can also try the recipes as they are in this book, If you are not sure, reduce the cooking time slightly, you can always cook a little longer if needed. Experimenting with different times and methods was fun for me and I hope it is the same for you.

Avocado Basil Salmon Cooked in Pressure Cooker (in foil)

Salmon, the delicate flavored fish, is a fish that is often included in different diets. This is because salmon is rich in protein, omega-3 fatty acids, and vitamin D, which is good for the heart and the body. In this recipe, the salmon is cooked with avocado and basil, flavors that will not overpower the delicate flavor of the fish, but will only enhance it.

Recipe: *Avocado Basil Steamed Pressure Cooked Salmon*

Cooking Time: *15 minutes*

Serves: *4*

Ingredients:

- Fresh Basil (chopped) - ½ cup
- Garlic (crushed) - 3 cloves
- Ripe Avocado - 1.
- Capers (drained and finely chopped) - 1 Teaspoon
- Lemon Zest - 1 Tablespoon
- Salmon Fillets - 4 – 6 oz. filets.
- Coconut Oil – 2 Tablespoon (for greasing the foil
- ½ cup water or broth of your choice

Preparation:

Step 1: Spread coconut oil on 12"x 12" sheets of aluminium foil.

Step 2: Set pressure cooker to warm.

Step 3: Cut the avocado in half, de-pit and scoop out the avocado and place in a bowl.

Step 4: Mash the avocado until very creamy.

Step 5: Add the avocado to chopped capers, garlic, and basil and lemon zest and mix well in a bowl.

Step 6: Now, place each salmon fillet on a coconut oil greased foil sheet

Step 7: Spread the avocado topping over the top of the salmon.

Step 8: Be sure that the avocado coating is ¼ inch thick for thinner fillets and up to ½ inch thick for thicker salmon fillets.

Step 9: Now, close and seal the foil packets, making sure all the ends are sealed firmly.

Step 10: Add water or broth to the pressure cooker, place a trivet or rack in the cooker, if you don't have one place the packets in the liquid one on top of another

Step 11: Seal the lid and set timer for 8 minutes. Release pressure manually and remove packets from pressure cooker. Let cool for 5 minutes or if you like it cooked a little more...

Step 12: Broil the fish for 3-4 minutes until avocado topping starts to brown.

Step 13: Remove from oven.

Step 14: Serve hot.

Under Pressure Red Snapper (in foil)

Red Snapper is a very popular fish found in the South-eastern parts of the United States. This firm fish has a distinct flavor that can handle many different seasoning and spices, as well as subtle herbs, that makes it a perfect addition to any diet. The red snapper is low in saturated fat and sodium a good source of Vitamin B6, Vitamin B12, phosphorus and potassium, and a very good source of protein and selenium.

Recipe: *Baked Red Snapper*   ***Cooking Time:*** *15 minutes*

Serves: *4*

Ingredients:

- Red Snapper filets – 4-8 oz. each.
- Lemon (sliced into thin circles) –2.
- Fresh Parsley Sprigs - ¼ Cup
- 1/4 cup of lemon juice
- ½ cup of water

Preparation:

Step 1: Prepare 4 pieces of aluminium foil (12"x12")

Step 2: Spread olive oil in the middle of each sheet.

Step 3: Place three lemon slices on each foil sheet.

Step 4: Gently place the fish on top of the lemon slices.

Step 5: Sprinkle with parsley.

Step 6: Now put the remaining lemon slices over the top of the fish.

Step 7: Fold the tin foil over the fish and fold the ends completely to form a sealed envelope in which the fish can cook easily.

Step 8: Pour liquid into the pressure cooker and place a trivet or rack inside.

Step 9: Place the packets inside the pressure cooker on top of the trivet or rack.

Step 10: If you do not have a trivet or rack you can place the packets in the liquid, one on top of the other.

Step 11: Set the Pressure Cooker timer for 10-12 minutes depending on how you like your fish cooked. 10 minutes should be fine.

Step 12: Release the pressure manually, remove foil packs, slice open and let cool for a few minutes

Step 13: Place packets on plates, slice open the foil and .enjoy!

Warm Beef Stew

There is nothing that states comfort as well as a bowl of warm beef stew, especially on a cold winter night. The difference in this recipe is that the recipe only uses grass-fed beef, instead of regular beef (if available). Grass-fed beef is considered to be healthier than regular beef as it has slightly less total fat content than grain-fed beef, however, has more Omega-3 fatty acids and CLA, which are both very beneficial for health.

Recipe: *Warm Beef Stew*

Cooking Time: *30 min*

Serves: *4*

Ingredients:

- Grass-fed Beef Chuck (cut into 2 inch chunks) - 3 lbs.
- Extra Virgin Coconut Oil - 3 Tablespoons
- Yellow onions (medium, peeled, halved and sliced into ¼ inch semi-circles) - 2
- Carrots – 2 nos.
- Celery (roughly chopped into ½ inch rounds) - 8 stalks
- Parsnips (roughly chopped into ½ inch rounds) - 2
- Garlic (chopped) - 8 cloves
- Chicken Broth - 2 cups
- Dry Red Wine - 2 cups
- Tomato Paste - ½ can
- Bay Leaf - 1
- Rosemary - 1 sprig
- Fresh Thyme (chopped) -1 ½ Tablespoon

Preparation:

Step 1: Set pressure cooker to heat mode and add oil.

Step 2: After the oil heats up, add half of the beef to the oil and stir frequently until the beef turns light brown.

Step 4: Remove the beef from the pc and keep aside.

Step 5: Now add the remaining beef to the pc and cook till they turn brown.

Step 6: Remove from the pan and keep aside.

Step 7: Now add the onions, celery, parsnips, and garlic and fry by stirring constantly.

Step 8: Keep stirring till your vegetables are cooked and are becoming soft. Around 5 minutes.

Step 9: After the vegetables have cooked, add all the beef to the pot and stir.

Step 10: Now, add the liquids to the pressure cooker.

Step 11: Lock the lid and set the timer for 25 minutes.

Step 12: Reduce pressure naturally.

Step 13: let simmer in the pressure cooker for 5 minutes with lid off.

Step 14: Remove from the pressure cooker.

Step 15: Serve hot.

Strawberry Basil Marinated Chicken

If you're looking for a sweeter twist for your next chicken dish, try this sweet and herbaceous marinade. Prepare this marinate in advance so that your chicken can marinate in it for at least 1 hour before cooking.

Marinade Ingredients:

- 1 cup fresh sliced strawberries
- ½ cup grape seed oil
- Juice and zest of 1 lemon
- ¼ cup basil, packed
- 1 tsp salt
- 1 tsp black pepper

Marinade Preparation:

Step 1: Blend all ingredients in a food processor until smooth.

Step 2: Pour over meat in a zip-top bag or airtight container

Step 3: Marinate at least 1 hour.

Ingredients for Strawberry Basil Marinated Chicken:

- 2 Boneless skinless Chicken Breasts (less than 2" thick) marinated
- ½ tablespoon oil

- Salt and Pepper
- 1 cup of water or chicken broth
- Tin Foil

Preparation for Strawberry Basil Marinated Chicken:

Step 1: Cut 2 pieces of aluminium foil – about 12" x 12"

Step 2: Spread olive oil on each piece of foil

Step 3: Remove breasts from marinade and place on oiled foil.

Step 4: Pour excess marinade on each chicken breast.

Step 5: Add salt and pepper.

Step 6: Fold foil around chicken and seal the edges.

Step 7: Add liquid to the pressure cooker and trivet if available.

Step 8: Place packets in the pressure cooker and seal lid.

Step 9: Set timer for 8 minutes and release pressure manually.

Cauliflower Rice

Cauliflower is a wonderful vegetable that can act as a substitute for, potatoes and grains, or rice and quinoa. A perfect substitute for Paleo and Gluten Free Dieters. It is filled with nutrients, such as, vitamins C, K, and B6, folate, fiber, manganese, and phosphorus potassium. Since it has a natural flavor you can season it with many different types of spices and can be used as a side dish or a main course.

Recipe: Cauliflower Rice

Serves: 4

Cooking Time: 10 minutes

Ingredients:

- Cauliflower head – 1
- Coconut oil – 1 Tablespoon
- Salt as per taste
- Pepper as per taste
- 1 cup water

Preparation:

Step 1: Place the cauliflower under running water and dry on kitchen towel.

Step 2: Cut or break the cauliflower into medium florets.

Step 3: Using the shredder blade of a food processor, place the cauliflowers florets into the processor and pulse until the cauliflower achieves rice like consistency.

Step 4: Remove from food processor.

Step 5: Place steamer basket in pressure cooker or wrap the cauliflower in foil

Step 6: Set timer for 5 minutes and release pressure manually

Step 7: Now, add the salt, pepper and coconut oil to rice and mix well.

Step 8: Serve.

Arugula Pesto Chicken

Pesto is a very versatile sauce, and with a change in one simple ingredient, you can change the flavor to suit all types of vegetarian and non-vegetarian recipes. Arugula pesto is so easy to make that the entire recipe takes only 10 minutes. While, pesto is mostly used in pastas, it also goes deliciously with proteins, hummus, pizza or different types of meats. In this recipe, the pesto is served with succulent chicken. Since, arugula is rich in Vitamin C and Potassium, the recipe provides a healthy combination of proteins and vitamins.

Recipe: Arugula Pesto Chicken

Cooking Time: 30 minutes

Serves: 5

Ingredients:

Arugula Pesto

- Fresh Arugula - 4 cups
- Garlic Cloves - 6
- Extra Virgin Olive Oil - 4 Tablespoon
- Lemon Juice - 1 Teaspoon
- Salt - ¼ Teaspoon
- ½ cup water

Pesto Chicken

- Chicken Breasts (boneless, skinless) - 5 6-8 oz. pieces.
- Garlic Powder - 2 Teaspoon

- Paprika - 2 Teaspoon
- Ground Coriander - 1 Teaspoon
- Ground Cumin - 1 Teaspoon
- Fresh Cracked Pepper - ½ Teaspoon
- Salt - 1 Teaspoon

Preparation:

Step 1: Heat a non-stick skillet over medium heat with olive oil.

Step 2: Add garlic with its peel to the skillet.

Step 3: Stir or shake the skillet frequently so that the garlic cooks on all side.

Step 4: Cook until the garlic is starting to brown and has become soft.

Step 5: Now, remove the garlic from the skillet and keep it aside to cool.

Step 6: After the garlic cools, remove the peel and keep aside.

Step 7: In a food processor bowl, add the arugula leaves, olive oil, peeled garlic cloves, salt and lemon juice.

Step 8: Pulse until all the ingredients are well combined and formed into a smooth paste.

Step 9: Keep the arugula pesto aside to use later.

Step 10: In a medium sized bowl, mix together the garlic powder, paprika, ground coriander, ground cumin, pepper, and salt. Mix the ingredients.

Step 11: Add the chicken breasts to the spice mixture.

Step 12: Using your hands or tongs, toss the chicken in the spice mixture to ensure that all the pieces are well coated with the spice.

Step 13: Wrap each coated chicken breast securely in a piece of aluminium foil

Step 14: Add 1 cup of water and trivet to the pressure cooker

Step 15: Add the chicken packets to the pressure cooker

Step 16: Seal the lid and set the timer to 10 minutes

Step 17: Release pressure manually, remove packets, cut open and cool for a few minutes

Step 18: Top with the Arugula Pesto

Salmon Wine Fillets

If you are looking for a simple yet healthy recipe that can be done in just 20 minutes, then the Salmon wine fillets is the best recipe for you. The recipe incorporates salmon fish and wine making it a delicious main course that can be served to impromptu guests. This simple recipe follows one of the best ways to cook salmon, which is by poaching. Not only does poaching the salmon in wine help to retain the fish's subtle flavor, but also helps to infuse the flavor of the wine and seasoning within the fish. This cooking method also helps to retain all the beneficial oils that salmons are known for.

Recipe: Salmon Wine Fillets   *Cooking Time:* 20 minutes

Serves: 4

Ingredients:

- Salmon Fillets – 4 - 6 to 8 ounce filets
- Olive Oil – 1 Teaspoon
- Dry White Wine - 1/3 cup
- Fresh Thyme (chopped) - 1 Teaspoon
- Spinach – 8 ounces
- Onions – 1 sliced
- Salt as per taste

Preparation:

Step 1: Prepare 4 sheets of aluminium foil large enough to wrap the fish and contents.

Step 2: Pour some white wine in a bowl and place the filets in for 10 minutes

Step 3: Coat each piece of foil with a thin layer of olive oil and place the marinated filets on top

Step 4: Sprinkle the fresh thyme on each piece then add a few slices of onion and a small handful of spinach. Add salt

Step 5: Wrap the foil around the content making sure the edges are sealed well.

Step 6: Seal the lid and set the timer for 10 minutes.

Step 7: Release the pressure manually, cut open, cool and serve

Herbed Parchment Salmon

Salmon is loaded with omega-3s and protein, and it consistently ranks as one of the highest omega-3 foods. As salmon is an oily fish, it is advisable to keep the supplementary ingredients on the healthier side to balance the high-fat content of the salmon and make it a more nutritious meal. This recipe also follows a unique style of cooking in which the fish is steamed inside a parchment.

Recipe: *Herbed Parchment Salmon*   ***Cooking Time:*** *30 minutes*

Serves: *2*

Ingredients:

- Extra Virgin Coconut Oil – 2 Tablespoon
- Lemon Zest – 1
- Garlic (crushed) 4 cloves
- Fresh Dill - ½ cup
- Fresh Parsley - 1/3 cup
- Salt - ½ Teaspoon
- Ground Pepper - 1/4 Teaspoon
- Salmon Fillets – 2 pieces.

Preparation:

Step 1: In a food processor, add the lemon zest, fresh dill, and parsley.

Step 2: Pulse until all the leaves are finely chopped.

Step 3: In a separate bowl, place the coconut oil and add the herb mixture.

Step 4: Mix until all the ingredients are well combined with the help of a fork.

Step 5: Turn on Pressure Cooker.

Step 6: Prepare the envelope for the fish by placing a large sheet of tin foil or parchment paper on a baking sheet. The parchment paper or foil should measure a little over twice the length of your fish fillets placed side by side.

Step 7: Place the fillets in the middle of parchment paper or foil, leaving 4 inches of space around each fillet so that it can easily fold over the fish.

Step 8: Spoon a Tablespoon full of coconut oil herb mixture onto each fillet.

Step 9: Add 1 Tablespoon of water around the fillets.

Step 10: Fold parchment paper or foil to cover the fish than fold all open sides to form a seal.

Step 11: Place a rack or trivet in the pressure cooker.

Step 12: Seal lid and set timer for 10 minutes.

Step 13: Release pressure manually, open, cool for a few minutes and serve.

Amberjack (Whitefish) Tarragon Fillet

Amberjack Whitefish is a fish that is recommended to be included in various different types of diets as it has very few calories. Unlike salmon, the fish has very little oil and fat content. Amberjack has a soft flaky texture when cooked, and comes with a mild and gentle flavor. It is for this reason that it is best to keep the supplement ingredients to the minimal so that the ingredients do not overpower the mild sweetness of the fish.

Recipe: Amberjack (Whitefish) Tarragon Fillet

Cooking Time: 20 minutes   *Serves:* 2

Ingredients:

- Amberjack Fillets – 2 (substitute with any other whitefish)
- Fresh Tarragon (chopped) - ¼ cup
- Extra Virgin Coconut Oil - 2 Tablespoon
- Fresh lemon to garnish
- Salt as per taste
- ½ cup water

Preparation:

Step 1: Cut two pieces of aluminium foil about 12"x12".

Step 2: Spread olive oil and the foil and place the fish on the foil.

Step 3: Evenly coat the fish with tarragon leaves.

Step 4: Sprinkle salt on top of the fish, place a lemon slice on each.

Step 5: Wrap the fish in the foil to make sealed packets.

Step 6: Place the packets on a trivet or rack in the pressure cooker, seal the lid and set timer for 8 minutes.

Step 7: When time is up release pressure manually.

Step 8: Open packet, cool and Serve

Mustard Rosemary Roasted Chicken

Although, whole roast chicken is considered to be a traditional holiday meal, it is one recipe that does not need any occasion to prepare. Roasting a whole chicken might look a bit complicated, however, it is a simple and easy recipe as all you have to do is marinate the chicken and place it in the pressure cooker. This mustard rosemary chicken recipe primarily calls for fully pastured chicken as they are considered to be better than farm-raised poultry. These chicken are raised on open pasture with access to natural feed that allows the chicken to have a better texture and flavor to farm-raised poultry. The mustard and rosemary seasoning is perfect for the recipe.

Recipe: Mustard Rosemary Roasted Chicken

Cooking Time: 20 minutes

Serves: 4

Ingredients:

- Chicken (fully pastured, whole) – 3lbs.
- Extra virgin coconut oil - 2 Tablespoon
- Brown Mustard - 2 Tablespoon
- Fresh Rosemary (chopped) -1 ½ Tablespoon
- 1 cup chicken broth

Preparation:

Step 1: Turn on Pressure Cooker

Step 2: Wash the chicken in cold water, pat dry with paper towels, remove any giblets that are present in the chicken.

Step 3: Heat some coconut oil in a separate pan and add the mustard and rosemary. Mix well

Step 4: Baste the entire surface of the chicken with the mustard sauce with the help of a brush..

Step 5: Place the chicken in pressure cooker, add broth, lock the lid and set timer for 20 minutes. Release pressure manually.

Step 6: Remove from pc and serve hot. If you like the skin browned, place in broiler for 5 minutes.

Pressure Cooker Lamb Stew

Stews, especially lamb stews, can take hours to make on a normal gas or electric stoves. However now with the use of the simple pressure cooker, these stews can easily be made within an hour or even less. A stew made in a pressure cooker produces soft and succulent  meat with an extremely flavorful broth. In this recipe, the lamb is prepared with different kinds of vegetables, like, squash, onions and garlic, resulting in a delicious stew that can be had by itself or with accompaniments. The stew also adheres to the Paleo diet as it does not use any grains, wheat or dairy and only specifically uses grass-fed lamb.

Recipe: Pressure cooker Lamb Stew

Cooking Time: 25 minutes

Serves: 4

Ingredients:

- Grass-fed Lamb (cut into 1 inch cubes) - 2 lb.
- Acorn Squash - 1
- Carrots (large) – 3

- Yellow Onion (large) - 1
- Rosemary - 1 sprig
- Bay Leaf - 1
- Garlic (sliced) - 6 cloves
- Broth – ½ cup
- Salt - ½ Teaspoon

Preparation:

Step 1: Peel, seed and cube acorn squash. Keep aside.

Step 2: Slice the carrots into thick circles. Keep aside.

Step 3: Peel the onion, cut in half, and then slice into half circles. Keep aside.

Step 4: Now, in the pressure cooker, add the lamb, acorn squash, carrots, yellow onions, rosemary, bay leaf, garlic, broth, and salt.

Step 5: Set timer for 25 minutes. Release pressure naturally.

Step 6: After the stew is ready, ladle it into serving bowls

Greek Baked Chicken PC

This baked chicken recipe is an easy and quick to put together, and can make for a perfect mid-week meal when there is a shortage of time. The recipe has a Greek inspired flavor that goes very well with salad, simply steamed or roasted veggies, and cauliflower rice.

Recipe: Greek Baked Chicken PC   ***Cooking Time:*** *30 minutes*

Serves: *5*

Ingredients:

- Organic Chicken (cut into parts) - 3 lb.
- Lemon Zest – 1

- Garlic (crushed) - 4 cloves
- Dried Oregano - 1 Tablespoon
- Salt - 1/4 Teaspoon
- Extra Virgin Coconut Oil - 2 Tablespoons
- ½ Cup Chicken Stock

Preparation:

Step 1: Set Pressure Cooker to warm.

Step 2: Pat chicken dry with paper towel and place in a dish

Step 3: Combine lemon zest, garlic, oregano, and salt in a small bowl. Keep aside

Step 4: In a separate small pan, heat the coconut oil.

Step 6: Add the lemon juice spice mixture to the coconut oil and mix well.

Step 7: Now, pour the coconut oil mixture over the chicken and mix to coat the chicken pieces evenly.

Step 8: Place trivet or rack in pressure cooker and add stock.

Step 9: Arrange chicken in a single layer (if possible) on trivet or rack in pressure cooker

Step 10: Set timer for 15 minutes, Release pressure naturally.

Step 11: If you prefer the skin to be a little crispy or browned place in broiler for 5 minutes.

Step 12: Serve hot.

Poached Salmon Teriyaki

Salmon being a mild and sweet flavored fish is considered to be perfect accompaniment to many other recipes. This recipe has a hint of teriyaki flavors. The salmon is poached in orange juice allowing the fish to absorb the lovely citrus flavor and natural sweetness of the orange. Since the fish is filled with good fatty acids and Omega 3, it also becomes a quick nutritious meal that is suitable for all types of individuals.

Recipe: Poached Salmon Teriyaki   *Cooking Time:* 20 minutes

Serves: 3

Ingredients:

- Orange Juice - 1/2 cup
- Coconut Aminos - 3 Tablespoon
- Fresh Ginger (finely grated) - 1½ Teaspoon
- Garlic (crushed) - 3 cloves
- Salmon Fillets – 3 6-8 oz. pieces

Preparation:

Step 1: In a medium sized bowl, add the orange juice, coconut aminos, ginger, and garlic and mix well.

Step 2: Now, place the salmon fillets on to the bottom of a large bowl.

Step 3: Pour the orange juice mixture over the salmon and let it sit for 15 minutes.

Step 4: After 15 minutes, pour the orange juice mixture into the pressure cooker.

Step 5: Add the Salmon filets on a trivet in the pressure cooker or place directly in the liquid.

Step 6: Set the timer for 8 minutes and release the pressure manually.

Step 7: After the fish has cooked, remove from pressure cooker to a serving dish.

Step 8: Serve along with stir-fired vegetables

Asian Chicken Pad Thai

Following a diet that restricts wheat and grains, does not mean that individuals can never indulge in fast food and different cuisines like Chinese. Instead of completely forgoing favorite cuisines and recipes, individuals can easily change these recipes to suit and match their diet. The Asia Chicken Pad Thai is one recipe that leaves out the noodles and uses healthy alternatives, such as broccoli slaw in its place. The taste of the recipe is never compromised and by using healthy ingredients, the recipe will suit all types of dietary restrictions and needs.

Recipe: Asian Chicken Pad Thai

Cooking Time: 10 minutes

Serves: 3

Ingredients:

- Pastured Chicken meat (cut into small 1" chunks) - 1½ lb
- Extra virgin coconut oil - 5 Tablespoon
- Cloves garlic, finely chopped - 5 nos
- Fish Sauce - 3 Tablespoon
- Coconut Aminos - 1 Tablespoon
- Fresh lime juice - 4 Tablespoon
- Coconut Vinegar - ½ Tablespoon
- Chopped fresh cilantro - 5 Tablespoon
- Finely chopped Green onions - 4-5
- Broccoli slaw –12oz
- Medium carrots - 2

Preparation:

Step 1: Set pressure cooker on heat or sauté mode.

Step 2: Add oil and garlic, cook about 1 minute.

Step 3: Add the chicken.

Step 4: Cook for 2-3 minutes, stirring frequently, until lightly browned.

Step 5: Add fish sauce, coconut aminos, lime juice and vinegar.

Step 6: Add broccoli slaw and julienned carrot and sauté for 2 more minutes.

Step 7: Stir in and close lid.

Step 8: Set timer for 8 minutes and release pressure manually.

Step 9: remove and place in serving bowl.

Step 10: Toss or garnish with green onion and cilantro.

Snapper with Asian vegetables in a bag

Again, following a diet that restricts wheat and grains, does not mean that individuals can never indulge in fast food and different cuisines like Asian cusine. Instead of completely forgoing favorite cuisines and recipes, individuals can easily change these recipes to suit and match their diet. The Snapper with Asian Vegetables is one recipe that leaves out the noodles and uses healthy alternatives, such as broccoli slaw in its place. The taste of the recipe is never compromised and by using healthy ingredients, the recipe will suit all types of dietary restrictions and needs.

Serves: 4

Sauce ingredients:

- ½ cup sweet chili sauce
- 2 Tbsp. fig preserves
- 1 Tbsp. coconut aminos
- 1 tsp garlic, chopped fine
- 1 tsp ginger, peeled & chopped fine
- 1/4 tsp Cajun seasoning

Fish ingredients:

- 4 sheets of parchment paper or aluminum foil (big enough to wrap fish)
- 12 oz. bag broccoli slaw

- 1 red or yellow pepper, seeded, sliced thin
- 4 each 5-6 oz. Snapper fillets, skinless
- Non-stick cooking spray or 4 tsps. olive oil
- Salt and pepper, optional

Preparation:

Step 1: Lay out the parchment paper or foil. Mix ingredients together to make Asian sauce.

Step 2: Spray each sheet of parchment paper lightly with non-stick cooking spray or tsp olive oil, one side only.

Step 3: Place broccoli slaw, peppers and 1/4 cup of the Asian garlic sauce in a bowl and stir well.

Step 4: Place 1/4 of the broccoli slaw mixture onto each of 4 of the parchment paper pieces. Top each with a piece of Snapper that has been seasoned with salt and pepper. Divide the remaining Asian garlic sauce between the 4 pieces of snapper.

Sealing the bag

Step 1: Seal the foil or parchment paper. Make sure all the edges are completely sealed.

Step 2: Place the packets on a trivet inside the pressure cooker with 2 cups of water, close lid.

Step 3: Set timer for 6 minutes. Release pressure when done, remove packets and serve.

Steak and Kidney Pie

One of the best ways to adapt traditional recipes like steak and kidney pies to different dietary needs and restrictions is by changing some small and simple ingredients in the recipe. In this version of the traditional steak and kidney pie, the traditional choux pastry has been left out. The recipe also uses grass-fed beef and pastured pork, making it a bit healthier and a suitable recipe for all types of individuals with different dietary needs.

Recipe: Steak and Kidney Pie

Cooking Time: 30 minutes

Serves: 8

Ingredients:

- Grass fed steak - 3 lbs
- Grass fed lamb kidney - 1 ½ lbs.
- Portobello mushrooms - 6 oz.
- Sweet onion - 1 large
- Bay leaf - 1
- Fish sauce - ½ Tablespoon
- Salt - ½ teaspoon
- Pepper - ½ teaspoon
- Medium carrots - 3
- Grass fed beef stock - 2 cups
- Arrowroot powder - 2 Tablespoon
- Pastured Bacon grease - 4 Tablespoon

Preparation:

Step 1: Slice grass fed steak and kidney into quarter inch thick slices.

Step 2: Slice carrot into half inch thick rounds.

Step 3: Slice Portobello mushrooms into half inch thick cubes.

Step 4: Cut onion in half and then slice into quarter inch thick half-moons.

Step 5: Heat 3 tablespoons of pastured bacon grease in pressure cooker.

Step 6: Brown grass fed meat and kidney separately in batches.

Step 7: Set aside.

Step 8: Add 1-2 tablespoons pastured bacon grease to pc pan if needed.

Step 9: Brown onion slices for 5-6 minutes.

Step 10: Add carrot and mushrooms for 3-4 more minutes.

Step 11: Return grass fed meat to the pc pot.

Step 12: Whisk arrowroot powder into grass fed beef stock and add to pot.

Step 13: Also add fish sauce and bay leaf.

Step 14: Set timer for 25 minutes.

Step 15: Release pressure naturally.

Step 16: Pour into a large casserole dish and serve.

Baked Mustard Lime Chicken

Among most meat and poultry, chicken is considered to be the lighter and healthier poultry food. Chicken, unlike red meat, is full of good protein and has very little cholesterol and fat. Individuals can make a recipe a bit healthier by using pastured chicken, instead of farm fed ones. Pastured chickens are considered to be a better option to farm fed ones, as pastured chicken are fed fresh grass and organic feed that is void of any anti-biotic. The chicken is also allowed free to roam on farms, which helps them to have less fat content than farm-fed chicken. This recipe for chicken breast is a flavorful recipe that uses lime and cilantro to bake the chicken in.

Recipe: *Baked Mustard Lime Chicken*

Cooking Time: *30 minutes*

Serves: *4*

Ingredients:

- Pastured Chicken Breast (skinless boneless) - 2 lbs. 4 pieces
- Fresh Lime Juice - ½ cup
- Fresh Cilantro (Chopped) - ½ cup
- Dijon Mustard - ¼ cup
- Olive Oil - 1 tablespoon
- Chili Powder - 1 tablespoon
- Celtic Sea Salt - ½ teaspoon
- Pepper - ½ teaspoon

Preparation:

Step 1: Combine lime juice, cilantro, mustard, olive oil, chili, salt and pepper in a food processor

Step 2: Pulse until ingredients are well combined

Step 3: Rinse chicken breasts, pat dry and place in a deep bowl.

Step 4: Pour marinade over chicken, cover and refrigerate for at least 15 minutes or up to 6 hours

Step 5: After the chicken has marinated, pour the marinade mixture into the pressure cooker.

Step 6: Add the chicken breasts and lock the lid. Set timer for 10 minutes. Release pressure manually.

Step 7: Serve with extra sauce spooned over top.

Roasted Herb Crusted Pork Loin

The Herb Crusted Pork Loin is a simple and flavorful recipe. This recipe follows a traditional method of cooking pork, which is by coating it with herbs and then slow roasting the pork meat but here we use a pressure cooker which reduces the cooking time. The recipe primarily uses pastured pork meat, which is considered to be tastier and healthier than farm bred pigs. The recipe will also suit all types of dietary restrictions and needs and diets as it uses Pork Loin, which is a lean meat.

Recipe: Roasted Herb Crusted Pork Loin

Cooking Time: 1 hour

Serves: 5

Ingredients:

- Pastured Pork Center Loin - 4 lb.
- Fresh Rosemary - 2 large sprigs
- Fresh Thyme - 12 sprigs
- Salt - ½ Teaspoon
- Pepper cracked - ½ Teaspoon
- Fresh Garlic - 9 cloves
- Lemon Zest - 2 Teaspoon
- Paprika - ½ Teaspoon
- ½ Cup Stock or Water

Preparation:

Step 1: In your blender, place the rosemary, thyme, salt, pepper, lemon zest, paprika, and fresh garlic.

Step 2: Blend the spices until they have combined completely.

Step 3: Now, using your hands rub the entire mixture over the pork loin. Ensure that the cut is evenly coated.

Step 4: Now, wrap the roast in a clear wrap and place it in the fridge for 1 hour.

Step 5: Remove from fridge, unwrap and place the roast fat side up on a trivet in the pressure cooker.

Step 6: Add the liquid, close the lid and set timer for 20 minutes. Reduce pressure naturally.

Step 7: Remove from cooker, slice and serve or place under broiler for 5 minutes, then serve.

Tarragon Salmon with Lemon

If you are looking for a quick, healthy and yet sophisticated recipe to serve impromptu guests, then the Tarragon Salmon with lemon is the one for you. With only a few ingredients, the recipe takes only 20 minutes to complete. Since, the recipe uses salmon as its main ingredients, the sweet flavor of the salmon is the highlight of the dish, which is only enhanced by the ingredients used in it. The recipe is extremely flavorful and is also quite healthy making it suitable for guests with dietary restrictions. Compliment it with Cauliflower Rice.

Recipe: *Tarragon Salmon with Lemon*

Cooking Time: *20 minutes*

Serves: *4*

Ingredients:

- Salmon steaks or fillets – 6 pieces.
- Fresh finely chopped tarragon - 2 Tablespoon
- Lemon zest - 2 Tablespoon
- Salt, to taste - 1/8 Teaspoon
- Cracked or ground pepper - 1/4 Teaspoon
- ½ cup water

Preparation:

Step 1: Add water to pressure cooker

Step 2: Line tin foil or parchment paper with olive oil or avocado oil.

Step 3: Combine the finely chopped tarragon, lemon zest, salt and pepper, in a small bowl.

Step 4: If salmon has skin on one side, place the skin side down on the foil or parchment paper.

Step 5: Sprinkle seasoning over the top of the salmon.

Step 6: Fold the foil or parchment paper making a closed packet.

Step 7: Place packets on rack in pressure cooker.

Step 8: Set timer for 6 - 10 minutes depending on how you like your salmon cooked.

Step 9: Release pressure manually, remove packets, let cool and serve.

Shrimp and Tilapia Seafood Curry

For many individuals, Tilapia whitefish is a health food that lacks in flavor. What many individuals do not realize is that the Tilapia is anything but boring. Unlike many other fishes, the Tilapia is one fish whose flavor shines in different types of ingredients. In this recipe, the Tilapia is used along with a variety of vegetables and spices primarily to add flavor and texture. The recipe also calls for coconut butter or coconut cream concentrate that gives the fish a bold flavor, which is backed by the underlying richness of coconut milk cream. Another great aspect about the Tilapia fish is that it is low in sodium and is a good source of Niacin and Phosphorus, and a very good source of Protein, Vitamin B12 and Selenium. Cooking it all together in a foil wrap makes it a complete meal ready to eat out of the packet in 10 minutes!

Recipe: *Tilapia Vegie Steam Pack*

Cooking Time: *20 minutes*

Serves: *2*

Ingredients:

- Tilapia Fillets - 2 fillets
- Cabbage (shredded) - 1 cups
- Carrots (medium) - 2
- Fresh Spinach (chopped) - 4 cups
- Chicken Broth - 1 cup

- Extra Virgin Coconut Oil - 2 Tablespoon
- Mushrooms sliced - 2
- Lemons - 2
- Salt to taste - ½ teaspoon
- Coconut Cream Concentrate - ¼ cup
- Fresh garlic – 2 chopped

Preparation:

Step 1: Shred cabbage into ¼ inch strips. Keep aside.

Step 2: Grate carrots with a coarse grater and keep aside.

Step 3: Place the Tilapia on a foil sheet coated with coconut oil and top with coconut cream.

Step 4: Put an equal amount of all the cut up vegies on top of the filets including the garlic.

Step 5: Top with lemon slices and fold the foil over the fish and vegies making a sealed packet.

Step 6: Pour chicken broth in the pressure cooker.

Step 7: Place packets in cooker

Step 8: Set timer for 10 minutes and then release pressure manually.

Step 9: Remove packets, place on plates and slice the foil to release the steam.

Chicken Italian in Foil

If you're looking for Italian twist for your next chicken dish, try this Italian favorite complete meal pack. Look for organic pasteurized chicken breasts and organic local grown vegetables.

Again, you can change it up to suit your tastes.

Serves: 2

Ingredients:

- Olive Oil and Apple Cider Vinegar
- 2 chicken breasts
- 1/4 tsp. salt

- med. zucchini, sliced
- 1 med. Onion sliced
- 2 tbsp. organic tomato sauce
- ½ tsp. oregano leaves
- 1 tbsp. coconut oil
- ½ cup mushrooms
- ½ cup green olives
- ½ cup water

Preparation:

Step 1: Brush Olive Oil and Apple Cider Vinegar on chicken.

Step 2: Sprinkle with salt. Cut zucchini into slices.

Step 3: Cut onion and salt.

Step 4: Place chicken pieces on zucchini and onion; top with tomato sauce, oregano and coconut oil. Sprinkle on olives.

Step 5: Wrap tightly in foil.

Step 6: Place trivet in pressure cooker, add ½ cup of water and lock lid.

Step 7: Set timer for 10 minutes and release pressure manually

Step 8: Transfer to plate, cut open foil and remove contents to plate, or eat directly from foil.

Spinach-Ham Frittata

Here is a quick meal you can have any time of the day although it is a preferable breakfast meal.

Prep Time: *20 minutes*
Total Time: *30 minutes*
Yield: *8 servings*

Ingredients:

- 8 large organic eggs, beaten
- 2 c. spinach, chopped
- 2 cloves garlic
- 1 c. ham, diced
- 1 small white onion, diced
- ½ c. canned coconut milk
- 1 tsp. coconut oil
- 1 tsp. sea salt
- ½ tsp. fresh ground black pepper

Preparation:

Step 1: Place the coconut oil into the pressure cooker and set on heat or sauté. Add in garlic and onion and sauté for 8 to 10 minutes or until the garlic becomes fragrant and the onion tender and translucent.

Step 2: Now add in chopped spinach and diced ham.

53

Step 3: In a medium-sized mixing bowl, whisk together eggs, coconut milk, sea salt, and pepper.

Step 4: Pour egg-mixture in the pressure cooker and stir to mix well with contents. Cover with lid and lock set the timer for 10 minutes.

Step 5: When ready release pressure manually open lid and scoop onto serving dish. Serve hot.

Paleo Chicken Curry

Eating Paleo is said to be boring by some people, but with recipes like Paleo Curry Chicken you almost forget about any restrictions and can enjoy many flavorful meals of different ethnicity. Remember the first choice is to use grass feed free range chicken and organic veggies.

Prep Time: *15 minutes*

Total Time: *25 minutes*

Yield: *4 servings*

Ingredients:

- 2 pounds boneless, skinless chicken breast, cut into 1-inch cubes.
- 2 cans of coconut milk
- ½ cup chicken broth
- 2 tbsp. red curry paste
- 1 small yellow onion, chopped into 1-inch cubes
- ½ medium red bell pepper, chopped into 1-inch cubes
- ½ medium green bell pepper, chopped into 1-inch cubes
- ¼ head of cauliflower, chopped
- ¼ head of cabbage, chopped
- 2 – 3 cloves garlic, minced (depending on preference of taste

Preparation:

Step 1: Set pressure cooker to heat or sauté before prepping ingredients.

Step 2: Prepare ingredients as instructed.

Step 3: Combine coconut milk and chicken broth in pressure cooker. Stir.

Step 4: Add red curry paste and stir.

Step 5: Place cauliflower in pressure cooker. Stir.

Step 6: Place chopped onion and red & green bell pepper in pressure cooker. Stir.

Step 7: Place chicken in pressure cooker and stir.

Step 8: To prepare cabbage. Take ¼ head of cabbage and cut into thin strips and separate. Add strips to cooker. Stir.

Step 9: Add 2 cloves of minced garlic, stir. Add more minced garlic, if needed, for taste.

Step 10: Cover pressure cooker with lid locked and set timer for 10 minutes.

Step 11: When ready, stir the chicken curry, transfer to serving bowl and serve hot.

Raspberry Beef Chili

Here is a real twist on a classic dish. Use your imagination and your pressure cooker and any meal requirements can be met and enjoyed.

Prep Time: *15 minutes*
Total Time: *35 minutes*
Yield: *4 servings*

Ingredients:

- 3-pounds grass-fed ground beef
- 1-pound ground liver
- 3 cans (14.5-ounces) diced tomatoes
- 2 cans (6-ounces) organic tomato paste
- 1-pound fresh raspberries
- 2 orange bell peppers, diced
- 2 chili peppers, deseeded and diced
- 2 Italian squash
- 3 cloves garlic, minced (or use 2 tbsp. garlic powder)
- 2 tbsp. paprika
- 1 tbsp. cumin
- 1 tbsp. dried oregano
- 1 tbsp. dried basil
- 1 tsp. fresh ground black pepper
- ¼ tsp. chili powder

- 1 tsp. cayenne pepper (to taste)
- 1 tbsp. dried basil
- 1 tsp. fresh ground black pepper
- ¼ tsp. chili powder
- 1 tsp. cayenne pepper (to taste
- ½ cup of water or broth

Preparation:

Step 1: Place the ingredients in your pressure cooker in the order listed. Stir contents until well blended.

Step 2: Cover cooker with lid and set timer for 20 minutes. Release pressure manually.

Step 3: To serve, transfer to serving bowl. Sprinkle on a pinch of sea salt, to taste (opt.)

Indian Chicken Curry

Eating Paleo is said to be boring by some people, but with recipes like Indian Curry Chicken you almost forget about any restrictions and can enjoy many flavorful meals of different ethnicity. Remember the first choice is to use grass feed free range chicken and organic veggies.

Ingredients:

- Chicken- 1 whole
- Coriander seeds- 1 teaspoon
- Spanish onion- 1
- Grated Ginger- 1 teaspoon
- Garlic Powder- 1 teaspoon
- Garam Masala Powder- 2 teaspoons
- Chili Powder- 1 teaspoon
- Oil- To tablespoons
- Salt to taste
- Cilantro to Garnish
- 1 cup water

For the Marinade
- Chili Powder- 1 teaspoon
- Turmeric Powder- ½ teaspoon
- Ginger Powder- 2 teaspoons
- Coriander Powder- 2 teaspoons

- Juice of 1 lemon
- Salt to taste.

Preparation:

Step 1: Marinade the chicken, cover and refrigerate for about 1 hour.

Step 2: Meanwhile, set the cooker to sauté or heat mode.

Step 3: Add the coriander seeds. Let the cook till they pop.

Step 4: Now add chopped onion and sauté till it is translucent.

Step 5: Add the garlic powder, garam masala, ginger powder and chili powder. Sauté for a minute.

Step 6: Add the tomatoes and cook them till they are soft.

Step 7: Add the marinated chicken and continue to sauté for 2 minutes.

Step 8: Add water and salt.

Step 9: Close the lid, lock it into place, close the vent and set timer for 20 minutes. (in poultry mode)

Step 10: When time is up, allow pressure to reduce naturally

Step 11: When pressure is reduced, open the lid and remove

Kosher Brisket Cooked in Chicken Broth

Ingredients:

- Kosher Brisket- 2-3 pounds
- Oil- 2 tablespoons
- Pepper- ½ teaspoon
- Spanish Onion- 1 medium sized
- Sweet potatoes- 5
- Baby carrots- 1 cup
- Chicken Broth- 1 ½ cups

Preparation:

Step 1: Set the cooker to the sauté mode.

Step 2: Add 1 tbsp. of oil to caramelize the onions. When the onions are golden brown, take them out and place them in a bowl

Step 3: Let the cooker stay in the sauté mode.

Step 4: Season the brisket with pepper on both sides. You may add salt if required.

Step 5: In the cooker, sear the beef.

Step 6: Then, throw in the carrots, sweet potatoes and onions.

Step 7: Pour the chicken broth over.

Step 8: Close the lid, lock it into place, close the vent and set timer for 40 minutes.

Step 9: When time is up, allow pressure to reduce naturally.

Step 10: When pressure is reduced, open the lid and remove all the vegetables.

Step 11: Put the cooker back on sauté mode and reduce the juices around the brisket to half.

Step 12: Once this is done, serve with the sides.

Healthy Mediterranean Fish

Here is a very healthy and easy pressure cooker recipe that is gluten free and Paleo compliant.

Ingredients:

- Fish Fillets- 4
- Cherry Tomatoes- 1 lb.
- Salt Cured Olives- 1 cup
- Pickled capers- 2 tablespoons

- Olive Oil
- Pressed Garlic- 1 clove
- Salt and Pepper

Preparation:

Step 1: Pour ½ cup water or broth in pressure cooker

Step 2: In a heat proof bowl, place the cherry tomatoes olives and the capers.

Step 3: Place the fish filets over the tomatoes olives and the capers

Step 4: Sprinkle with garlic, olive oil and salt and pepper.

Step 5: Place the bowl inside the pressure cooker.

Step 6: Close the lid, lock it into place, close the vent and set timer for 8 minutes.

Step 7: When time is up, reduce pressure manually.

Step 8: When pressure is reduced, open the lid and carefully remove the fish fillets.

Step 9: Plate the fish and top with the tomatoes, olives and capers

Step 10: Your dish is ready to be served

Steak Pizzaiola

If you like a nice steak (grass feed) with an Italian flair that cooks quickly in your pressure cooker try this one.

Cooking steak this way can be a little tricky till you get the hang of it and figure out how long your pressure cooker needs to cook the steak to your liking.

Servings: 6

Ingredients:

- 2 lbs. flank steak, sliced
- ½ lbs. sliced mushrooms

- 2 tbsp. olive oil
- 1 onion, sliced
- 2 bell peppers, chopped
- 1 (14 oz.) can crushed tomatoes (organic)
- 1 tbsp. minced garlic
- 2 tsp. dried basil
- Salt and pepper to taste

Preparation:

Step 1: Heat the oil in the pressure cooker on the "sauté or heat" setting.

Step 2: Add the sliced beef and cook until browned. Set aside.

Step 3: Add the onions and cook until softened, about 2 minutes.

Step 4: Add in the mushrooms, crushed tomatoes, garlic, peppers and spices. Stir to combine.

Step 5: Return the meat to the pressure cooker and close and lock the lid.

Step 6: Set timer for 25 minutes. Release pressure naturally

Step 7: Remove the lid and stir. Serve hot.

Lemon Chicken with Herbs

All natural clean ingredients makes this a tasty lemony dish ths is quick to prepare in your pressure cooker.

Servings: 4

Ingredients:

- 4 boneless chicken breasts, cubed
- ½ cup white wine
- 2 tbsp. olive oil

- 2 tbsp. fresh lemon juice
- 2 tsp. minced garlic
- 2 tsp. chicken bouillon granules
- 1 tbsp. fresh chopped basil
- 1 tbsp. fresh chopped oregano
- Salt and pepper to taste

Preparation:

Step 1: Heat the olive oil in the pressure cooker on the "sauté or heat" setting.

Step 2: Add the chicken and cook until evenly browned.

Step 3: Stir in the remaining ingredients and close and lock the lid.

Step 4: Set the timer for 8 minutes.

Step 5: Release pressure manually.

Step 6: Remove the lid and transfer the chicken to a platter.

Step 7: Simmer the sauce on the "heat" setting for 5 minutes or until slightly thickened.

Step 8: Serve hot with the chicken.

Basil Tomato Chicken

Here is another quick and healthy recipe that infuse an Italian flavor directly into the chicken breast as it cooks and leaves a nice flavorful sauce to top it off.

Servings: 4

Ingredients:

- 4 boneless chicken breasts
- 2 tbsp. olive oil
- 1 chopped onion
- 1 (28 oz.) can organic Italian stewed tomatoes
- ¼ cup fresh chopped basil
- 2 tsp. minced garlic
- Salt and pepper to taste

Preparation:

Step 1: Rub the chicken with pepper and salt on both sides.

Step 2: Heat the olive oil in the pressure cooker on the "sauté or heat" setting.

Step 3: Add the chicken and cook until evenly browned. Set aside.

Step 4: Put in the garlic and onions, stir and cook for 2 minutes or until tender.

Step 5: Add the remaining ingredients and return the chicken to the cooker.

Step 6: Close and lock the lid in place.

Step 7: Set timer for 8 minutes. Allow the cooker to depressurize naturally.

Step 8: Remove the lid and transfer the chicken to a platter.

Step 9: Serve hot with the sauce on top.

Chicken and Sweet Potato Stew Recipe

A very nice stew recipe using sweet potatoes in place of regular potatoes. Fun to prepare and very tasty.

Servings: 4

Ingredients:

- 6 bone-in chicken thighs (remove skin and trim fat)
- ½ pound white button mushrooms, thinly sliced
- 6 large shallots, peeled, halved
- 4 cloves garlic, peeled
- 1 cup dry white wine
- 1 ½ tablespoons white wine vinegar
- 2 teaspoons chopped fresh rosemary
- 1 teaspoon salt
- ½ teaspoon freshly ground pepper

Preparation:

Step 1: Rub the chicken with pepper and salt on both sides.

Step 2: Heat the olive oil in the pressure cooker on the "sauté or heat" setting.

Step 3: Add the chicken and cook until evenly browned.

Step 4: Add sweet potatoes, mushrooms, shallots, garlic, wine, rosemary, salt and pepper to the pressure cooker and stir to combine.

Step 5: Close and lock the lid in place.

Step 6: Set timer for 8 minutes. Allow the cooker to depressurize naturally.

Step 7: Remove the lid and transfer the chicken to a platter

Step 8: Debone the chicken and stir into the pressure cooker adding white wine vinegar.

Step 9: Remove contents to platter and serve.

Chicken with zucchini spaghetti and tomato

If you like all in one meals this is healthy one that is quick to prepare.

Servings: 4

Ingredients:

- 4 thin (1') Chicken Breasts
- 1 green zucchini julienned (spaghetti sized long, thin)
- 2 onions sliced
- 2 sliced tomatoes
- 1 cup water or broth
- 1 tablespoons olive oil.
- 1 teaspoons basil
- 1 teaspoon salt
- ½ teaspoon freshly ground pepper

Preparation:

Step 1: Place each chicken breast on a 12x12 piece of aluminium foil.

Step 2: Place chicken breast in the center of each foil.

Step 3: Top chicken with ¼ tablespoon olive oil, salt, pepper. Sprinkle basil over the top.

Step 4: Place 2 slices of tomato and 1 slice of onion over chicken.

Step 5: Put a heap of julienned zucchini on top.

Step 6: Wrap chicken in a secure sealed packet.

Step 7: Add water or broth to pressure cooker.

Step 8: Place packets into pressure cooker.

Step 9: Close and lock the lid in place.

Step 10: Set timer for 10 minutes. Release pressure naturally.

Step 11: Remove the lid and carefully remove hot packets.

Step 12: Slice open packet to cool.

Step 13: Eat directly out of packet.

Moroccan Chicken

For another ethnic flavorful dish this Morocan Chicken uses lots of spice to infuse the flavor into the chicken.

Servings: *4*

Ingredients:

- 1 Whole organic chicken cut into parts.
- 1 teaspoon paprika
- ¼ teaspoon ground turmeric.
- 1 teaspoon quick cook tapioca
- ½ cup of black olives.
- 1 large onion chopped.
- ½ cup of black olives.
- 1 teaspoon of fresh cilantro, chopped.
- 2 garlic cloves, minced.
- 1 cup water or broth
- 2 tablespoons extra virgin olive oil.
- 1 lemon, juice and zest.
- 1 teaspoon kosher salt
- ½ teaspoon freshly ground pepper

Preparation:

Step 1: Season chicken with salt and pepper.

Step 2: Set pressure cooker to sauté or heat mode.

Step 3: heat olive oil and brown chicken pieces in pressure cooker along with onion and garlic.

Step 4: Combine the lemon, paprika, turmeric, tapioca and olives in a bowl.

Step 5: Add ½ cup or water or organic chicken broth

Step 6: Pour the ingredients from the bowl over the chicken.

Step 7: Close and lock the lid in place.

Step 8: Set timer for 20 minutes. Release pressure naturally.

Step 9: Remove the lid and carefully transfer to serving dish.

Very Veggie Chicken

An all in one meal that uses coconut aminos to add a great flavor to a big selection of vegetables to top the chicken breasts. The cooking can be tricky depending on the thickness of the breasts (I use thin 1" breasts) and the way you prefer the chicken. Try this as it is, it should be perfect.

Servings: 4

Ingredients:

- 4 thin Chicken Breasts – 1 to 2" thick.
- 1 cup sliced mushrooms
- 2 onions diced

- 1 cup coconut aminos
- 1 cup grape tomatoes
- 1 cup water or broth
- 1 tablespoons olive oil.
- 1 yellow squash thin sliced
- 1 cup broccoli florets
- 1 cup spinach
- 1 teaspoon salt
- ½ teaspoon freshly ground pepper

Preparation:

Step 1: Place each chicken breast on a 12x12 piece of aluminium foil.

Step 2: Place chicken breast in the center of each foil.

Step 3: Top chicken with ¼ tablespoon olive oil, salt, pepper.

Step 4: Place 2 slices of tomato and diced onions and mushroom slices over chicken.

Step 5: Put a few round slices of squash and a few broccoli florets on top.

Step 6: Top each with a handful of spinach.

Step 7: Top spinach with a tablespoon of coconut aminos.

Step 8: Wrap chicken in a secure sealed packet.

Step 9: Add water or broth to pressure cooker.

Step 10: Place packets into pressure cooker on trivet or rack.

Step 11: Close and lock the lid in place.

Step 12: Set timer for 10 minutes. Release pressure manually.

Step 13: Remove the lid and carefully remove hot packets.

Step 14: Slice open packet to cool and eat.

Chicken and Spinach Curry

A different twist on a very healthy curry flavored dish with spinach and organic pasta sauce adding to the curry flavor.

Serves: 6

Ingredients:

- 2 lb boneless chicken breasts, skinned and chopped into 1" chunks.
- 2 (10 oz each) packages frozen spinach, thawed
- 2 tbsp. organic sugar free apple sauce
- ½ cup chicken broth
- 1 tbsp. mild curry powder
- 1 ½ cups organic sugar free pasta sauce
- Salt and freshly ground black pepper to taste
- Chopped fresh cilantro, for garnishing

Preparation:

Step 1: Set cooker to heat or sauté, add Olive Oil to the pressure cooker and brown chicken lightly.

Step 2: Leave the chicken pieces in the pressure cooker and pour in the broth

Step 3: Scatter the spinach leaves on top.

Step 4: Whisk the curry powder into the pasta sauce until well mixed and drizzle it over the spinach.

Step 5: Don't stir and secure the lid.

Step 6: Set the timer for 5 minutes.

Step 7: Release the pressure by fast release method and unlock the cooker.

Step 8: Spoon in the applesauce and stir all together to mix well.

Step 9: Simmer the sauce, uncovered, for about 5 minutes or until the sauce thickens slightly and adjust the seasonings.

Step 10: Sprinkle the chopped cilantro over each serving and serve warm.

Step 11: Serve with sautéed vegetables.

Mushroom Chicken

A combination of shiitake, button, crimini, and oyster. Make sure clean the mushrooms well.

Ingredients

- 5 cups sliced mixed fresh mushrooms
- 1 medium onion, chopped
- ½ cup chopped carrot
- 1/4 cup dried tomato pieces
- 3/4 cup chicken broth
- 1/4 cup dry white wine or water
- 3 tablespoons quick-cooking tapioca
- 1 teaspoon dried thyme, crushed
- ½ teaspoon dried basil, crushed
- ½ teaspoon garlic salt
- ½ teaspoon pepper
- 3 pounds chicken thighs or drumsticks (with bone), skinned
- 4 cups cooked spinach

Preparation:

Step 1: Place the mushrooms, onion, carrot, dried tomato, chicken broth, wine, tapioca, thyme, basil, garlic salt, and pepper into the pressure cooker and then top with the chicken.

Step 2: Cover the cooker and set timer for 10 minutes

Step 3: Serve the chicken over the spinach.

Sweetened Baked Acorn Squash

Nice sweet side dish that does use a bit of coconut sugar, but should be fine for Paleo

Recipe: *Sweetened Baked Acorn Squash*

Cooking Time: *20 minutes*

Serves: *2*

Ingredients:

- Golden Acorn Squash - 1 nos.
- Virgin Olive Oil - 2 Tablespoons

- Coconut Sugar - 2 Teaspoons
- Cinnamon Powder – 1 Teaspoon cinnamon
- One cup water.

Preparation:

Step 1: Take the Golden Acorn Squash and cut it in half.

Step 2: Remove all the seeds from the squash by gently scooping the seeds out with a spoon. Keep Aside.

Step 3: Now, with the help of a brush, evenly spread the olive oil onto each half of the squash. Remember to coat the exterior of the squash with oil as well.

Step 5: Add one tablespoon of coconut sugar to each half of the squash.

Step 6: Sprinkle ½ teaspoon of cinnamon powder on each half of the squash.

Step 7: Add the water and place each half of the squash in the pressure cooker.

Step 9: Close the lid, seal and set timer for 15 minutes

Step 10: Release pressure naturally.

Step 11: Remove from pressure cooker.

Step 12: Serve warm.

Butternut Squash Soup with an Apple Twist

The Butternut Squash Apple Soup is one of the best soups that can be made during the cold winter months. This simple and healthy recipe helps to spread warmth through the body with ingredients such as butternut squash and cinnamon powder. The recipe uses apples to give a twist to the traditional  butternut squash soup, which acts as the perfect flavor enhancer as the sweetness of the butternut squash pairs perfectly with the tartness of the apples. Being a versatile recipe, which is absolutely gluten-free, grain-free and dairy free, the soup can be served on special occasions, as well as, for a small dinner at home.

Recipe: Butternut Squash Soup with an Apple Twist

Cooking Time: 30 minutes

Serves: 4

Ingredients:

- Yellow Onion (diced) - 1 nos.
- Garlic (minced) - ½ Teaspoon1 rib celery, chopped
- Carrot (chopped) - 1

- Olive Oil - 1 Tablespoon
- Butternut Squash (peeled seeded and chopped) – 1.
- Apple (peeled, cored and chopped) - 1
- Chicken Broth (low sodium and gluten free) - 3 Cups (Substitute with vegetable broth)
- Cinnamon Powder - ¼ Teaspoon
- Nutmeg Powder - 1/8 Teaspoon
- Salt and Pepper as per taste

Preparation:

Step 1: Set pressure cooker to heat or sauté mode, add the olive oil and heat it for 5 minutes.

Step 2: Now, add the onion, garlic, celery, and carrot to the cooker pan and stir for 5 minutes, or until the onion turn translucent.

Step 3: Add the squash, apple and chicken broth into the pressure cooker and stir so that all the ingredients are combined well.

Step 4: Set the timer for 15 minutes then release pressure manually.

Step 5: After the soup cools, pour it into a food processor and blend into a smooth consistency.

Step 6: Pour in bowls and serve.

Balsamic Chicken and Sausages

This dish comes with an overdose of meat thus making it perfect for hardcore carnivores. It's bursting with a cocktail of tart and aromatic flavors which embrace the juicy chicken and sausages to spell sheer magic. Yet its 100% Paleo and don't pose a threat to your health!

Serves: 4-6

Ingredients:

- 6 fresh Italian sausage links
- 4-6 boneless and skinless chicken breasts
- 2 cans (14.5 oz.) diced tomatoes
- 4-6 garlic cloves, chopped
- 1 white onion, thinly sliced
- 1 can (15 oz.) tomato sauce
- ½ cup balsamic vinegar
- 1½ tsp garlic powder
- 2 tsp Italian seasoning
- 1½ tsp kosher salt
- Extra virgin olive oil, as required
- 1 cup home-made no-salt chicken stock

Preparation:

Step 1: Place the chicken breasts in pressure cooker and slather them with 2 tbsp. olive oil.

Step 2: Sprinkle a tsp each of garlic powder, Italian seasoning and kosher salt over them; don't stir.

Step 3: Arrange the sausage links on top of the chicken, followed by onion slices and chopped garlic.

Step 4: Empty the can of diced tomatoes into the pressure cooker and pour in the tomato sauce.

Step 5: Add the chicken stock as well as balsamic vinegar into the cooker and sprinkle the rest of seasonings on top; don't stir.

Step 6: Fasten the lid and set timer for 15 minutes.

Step 7: Serve hot with spaghetti squash and enjoy!

Mongolian Beef

Though yummy, Chinese take outs are loaded with unhealthy non-Paleo ingredients, thus making it a strict no-no for health buffs. So why not replicate the same flavors in your kitchen while sticking to Paleo norms to make sure it's healthy and delicious all at once!

Serves: 4

Ingredients:

- 2 lb. beef round steak, thinly sliced
- 5-6 green onions, chopped
- 2 tsp grated ginger
- 5 garlic cloves, minced
- 2 carrots, chopped into bite-sized chunks
- ½ cup arrowroot powder
- ½ cup coconut aminos
- ¼ cup beef broth
- 2 tbsp honey
- 2 tsp rice wine vinegar
- 1 tbsp. red chili paste
- 1 tsp molasses
- 2 tsp sesame oil
- 1 tbsp. almond butter
- ¼ tsp ground black pepper

Preparation:

Step 1: Spread the arrowroot powder in a shallow dish and place the beef slices on it.

Step 2: Flip them over to dredge well and shake off any excess; set aside.

Step 3: Dump rest of the ingredients into the pressure cooker and stir them all together to mix thoroughly.

Step 4: Arrange the dredged beef slices on top.

Step 5: Fasten the lid and set the timer for 25 minutes.

Step 6: Release pressure manually.

Step 7: Serve hot.

Step 8: Release pressure manually. Open lid and serve hot.

Honey-Garlic Chicken Wings

Cooking chicken wings in a crockpot gives you the chance to deal with a huge amount without sweating in the kitchen for long hours. And the outcome is always so juicy and lipsmacking! Indeed, it's hard to ignore the wonderful contrast of the sweetness of honey with the savory flavors.

Yields: 20-30 wings

Ingredients:

- 2-3 lb. chicken wings
- 1 ½ tbsp minced garlic
- ¾ cup raw honey
- ½ tsp freshly ground black pepper
- ½ tsp sea salt
- 2 tbsp. olive oil
- One cup water

Preparation:

Step 1: Arrange the chicken wings onto steamer basket in pressure cooker.

Step 2: Add one cup water.

Step 3: Close lid and set pressure cooker for 8 minutes.

Step 4: Release pressure manually

Step 5: Pour the honey in a bowl and whisk in olive oil, garlic as well as a dash of seasonings until they blend thoroughly.

Step 6: Remove wings from the cooker and put in the bowl.

Step 7: Mix the honey mixture over the wings and give them a good stir to coat evenly.

Step 8: Pace wings on a foil tray a place under broiler for 5 minutes.

Printed in Great Britain
by Amazon